D0998285

Sixty Poems of Martial

English versions by Dudley Fitts

THE LYSISTRATA OF ARISTOPHANES

THE FROGS OF ARISTOPHANES

THE BIRDS OF ARISTOPHANES

LADIES' DAY. THE THESMOPHORIAZÛSAE OF ARISTOPHANES

POEMS FROM THE GREEK ANTHOLOGY

By Dudley Fitts and Robert Fitzgerald

THE ALCESTIS OF EURIPIDES

THE ANTIGONE OF SOPHOCLES

THE OEDIPUS REX OF SOPHOCLES

Dudley Fitts

SIXTY POEMS OF MARTIAL

In Translation

Harcourt, Brace & World, Inc., New York

FIRST EDITION
Library of Congress Catalog Card Number: 67–19196
Printed in the United States of America

Many of these poems
have made a preliminary appearance
in the following magazines:
Accent;
The Atlantic Monthly;
Chicago Choice;
New World Writing;
Poetry ("Conversion," "'... Are Many Mansions,'"
"Society Note," "To His Critics");
Poetry London–New York;
Quarterly Review of Literature;
The Spider's Web
(Jonathan Edwards College, Yale University).

for Norman Holmes Pearson

–nos hæc novimus esse nihil

A Note on the Author and the Text

MARCUS VALERIUS MARTIALIS was born in Spain about the year 40 A.D., and died there some sixty years later. He was given an excellent education at home and at the age of twenty-three or thereabouts migrated to the Capital of the World, where he spent all but the last three or four years of his life. The details of his life in Rome are obscure in spite of his voluminous writings; but he seems to have made his way, precariously and with the customary disheartening sycophancy, under a series of emperors that included the ineffable Domitian, living by his wits and protected by his viciously sharp tongue. Apparently he never married—the 'Wife' of XI:104 being a dramatic fiction in the Browning manner; and the Marcella of whom he speaks affectionately late in life a wealthy patroness in his home town of Bilbilis, to which he returned to die—and little is known about his personal attachments. He was on familiar terms with Juvenal, Quintilian, Silius Italicus, and Pliny the Younger, but the evidence suggests that the familiarity was rather his than theirs.

His surviving works comprise fourteen books of Epigrams and a *Liber Spectaculorum* of thirty-two brief poems. In his hands the Epigram, a Greek form Latinized and already fashionable in his time, became a supple and deadly instrument of great range. An epigram need not always be destructive, and the majority of Martial's are harmlessly topical, small mirrors reflecting the trivialities of daily life. It is his destructive ones, however, that set his style and established a genre of personal and social satire that is still very much alive; and it is upon this acrid vein that I have drawn, making no apologies for slanting the evidence, in my brief selection. The translations, varying in style with the occasion and the mood, are free—sometimes very free—paraphrases of the original. The Latin text printed *en face* is based upon the Oxford edition of W. M. Lindsay (1902), though I have accepted a few later readings and generally lightened the punctuation.

DF

Contents

Sixty Poems of Martial

III:44

Occurrit tibi nemo quod libenter,
quod, quacumque uenis, fuga est et ingens
circa te, Ligurine, solitudo,
quid sit, scire cupis? Nimis poeta es.
hoc ualde uitium periculosum est.
non tigris catulis citata raptis,
non dipsas medio perusta sole,
nec sic scorpios inprobus timetur.
nam tantos, rogo, quis ferat labores?
et stanti legis et legis sedenti,
currenti legis et legis cacanti.
in thermas fugio: sonas ad aurem.
piscinam peto: non licet natare.
ad cenam propero: tenes euntem.
ad cenam uenio: fugas sedentem.
lassus dormio: suscitas iacentem.
Vis quantum facias mali uidere?
uir iustus probus innocens timeris.

To Ligurinus, Relentlessly a Poet

You ask me, friend, why nobody wants to meet you?
Why your very approach empties auditoriums?
Why, wherever you go,
you're the focus of a yawning wilderness?
Ligurine,
the reason's plain: you're much too much the poet.

That's a disastrous thing to be, worse
than a tigress roused by the miaous of her kidnapped kits,
worse than a sunstruck copperhead at noon,
worse than a hung-over scorpion.
Really, friend,
have you ever thought how much you ask of your public?

Let them be standing or sitting, you read them
your poetry. Let them run, not walk, to the exit, you
read them your poetry. The privy's no refuge, for there
you are, and you read them your poetry.
When I go
to one of the public baths, your voice is round me
like a bursting sea. I dive into the pool,
and lo thou art with me, chanting. I'm late for dinner:
you make me a canto's length later. I sit down to table,
you're reciting under the table. And I'd go to bed,
but you'd jerk me awake with a sonnet sequence.
No.
You're a kindly good man, Ligurine; but a calamity, too—
a poet wagged by a tongue in perpetual motion.

III:44

I:27

Hesterna tibi nocte dixeramus,
quincunces puto post decem peractos,
cenares hodie, Procille, mecum.
tu factam tibi rem statim putasti
et non sobria uerba subnotasti
exemplo nimium periculoso:
μισῶ μνάμονα συμπόταν, Procille.

To Procillus, Who Pours His Drinks into the Rubber Plant

It was after a couple of fifths of Old Fitz, Procillus,
or maybe Old Melody,
that my wife & I, reeling under your unexpected hos-
pitality, said
(and I think I quote):
'Procillus,
tomorrow the drinks are on us.'
(End quote.)
And you—
what did you do
but haul out your engagement book & write it down!
Au diable la mémoire des buveurs,
Procillus Pal.

I:27

VIII:54

Formonsissima quae fuere uel sunt,
sed uilissima quae fuere uel sunt,
o quam te fieri, Catulla, uellem
formonsam minus aut magis pudicam!

To Catulla

Loveliest of all women
                    living or dead,
vilest of all women
                    living or dead,
ah, dearest, that you were less lovely
or less vile.

VIII: 54

XII:20

Quare non habeat, Fabulle, quaeris
uxorem Themison? Habet sororem.

Themison's Got It Made

How to explain the fact that Mr
T.'s unmarried? He has a sr.

XII:20

X:68

Cum tibi non Ephesos nec sit Rhodos aut Mitylene,
  sed domus in uico, Laelia, patricio,
deque coloratis numquam lita mater Etruscis,
  durus Aricina de regione pater;
κύριέ μου, μέλι μου, ψυχή μου congeris usque,
  pro pudor! Hersiliae ciuis et Egeriae.
lectulus has uoces, nec lectulus audiat omnis,
  sed quem lasciuo strauit amica uiro.
scire cupis quo casta modo matrona loquaris?
  numquid, cum crisas, blandior esse potes?
tu licet ediscas totam referasque Corinthon,
  non tamen omnino, Laelia, Lais eris.

Local Products Preferred

Abigail, you don't hail from La Ville
Lumière, or Martinique, or even Québec, P.
Q., but from plain old Essex County;
Cape Ann, believe me, for ten
generations.
                    Accordingly, when
you gallicize your transports, such as they are,
and invoke me as *mon joujou!*, *petit
trésor!*, *vit de ma vie!*, I grow
restive.
            It's only bed-talk, I know,
but not the kind of bed-talk you
were designed for, darling.
                                        Let's you and me
go native. Damn your Berlitz. Please,
woman, you're an Abigail,
                                        not a *pièce exquise*.

x:68

XI:92

Mentitur qui te uitiosum, Zoile, dicit:
  non uitiosus homo es, Zoile, sed uitium.

Distinction

He's a liar, Zoïlus, who calls you a vicious man.
You're not a vicious man, you're Vice itself.

XI:92

VI:51

Quod conuiuaris sine me tam saepe, Luperce,
  inueni noceam qua ratione tibi.
Irascor: licet usque uoces mittasque rogesque—
  'Quid facies?' inquis. Quid faciam? ueniam.

The Ultimatum

You're always leaving me out
of your supper parties, Lupercus, but
I know a way to get back at you.

—What

's that?

—I'll blow my top. And you
can send me your invitations, and beg me,
implore me on bended knees.

—I see.

Then what'll you do?

—Do? Me?

I'll come to your party, naturally!

VI:51

VI:40

Femina praeferri potuit tibi nulla, Lycori:
  praeferri Glycerae femina nulla potest.
Haec erit quod tu: tu non potes esse quod haec est.
  Tempora quid faciunt! hanc uolo, te uolui.

Vicissitude

Lycóris,
no woman was dearer to me in those days
than you. Now Glýcera
takes my whole heart.
                                        Time's ways!
She'll be, I know, what now you are to me,
but you'll not be what she is.
                                                  Once
I longed for you, Lycóris.
                                             I long for her.

VI:40

X:16

Dotatae uxori cor harundine fixit acuta,
  sed dum ludit, Aper: ludere nouit Aper.

Bull’s-Eye

He aimed at the target, but he got
his wife in the gullet. Lucky shot.

x:16

III:8

'Thaida Quintus amat.' 'Quam Thaida?' 'Thaida luscam.'
Vnum oculum Thais non habet, ille duos.

Madrigal for Two Voices

'Q's in love with Lily.'
'Lily who?'
'Shy-an-eye Lily.'
'Q's shy two.'

III:8

I:38

Quem recitas meus est, o Fidentine, libellus:
sed male cum recitas, incipit esse tuus.

A Poetry Reading

Those are my poems you're reciting, Fidentinus,
but the way you garble them
makes them all your own.

1:38

XII:84

Nolueram, Polytime, tuos uiolare capillos,
sed iuuat hoc precibus me tribuisse tuis.
talis eras, modo tonse Pelops, positisque nitebas
crinibus ut totum sponsa uideret ebur.

Amende, of Sorts

Polytimus, what I said about your hair-cut
had no malice in it: not
for worlds would I question your taste. That
stripped dome, radiant, is mythical:
Pelops with his ivory shoulder
yields to you,
                    solid ivory skull.

XII:84

IV:38

Galla, nega: satiatur amor nisi gaudia torquent:
sed noli nimium, Galla, negare diu.

To His Mistress, That She Should Be Coy

Say No to my kiss, Francie: love's song
is queered by a facile counterpoint.
Only, dear Francie, don't say No too long.

IV:38

I:73

Nullus in urbe fuit tota qui tangere uellet
uxorem gratis, Caeciliane, tuam,
dum licuit; sed nunc positis custodibus ingens
turba fututorum est: ingeniosus homo es.

Negative Capability

There wasn't a man in town—believe me, Cecil,—
who'd have touched that wife of yours with a ten-foot pole
when she could be had for free;

                                        but now, Cecil,
what with the private eyes and the bugging and all,
your pad's awash with would-be co-respondents.

Cecil, man, you're immense!

I:73

III:42

Lomento rugas uteri quod condere temptas,
  Polla, tibi uentrem, non mihi labra linis.
simpliciter pateat uitium fortasse pusillum:
  quod tegitur, maius creditur esse malum.

To Polla, That She Should Leave Ill Enough Alone

With a viscid disaster of bean meal & rice
you plaster your poor torso.
                                        Polla, you don't
fool me a bit. What's a wrinkle between old friends?

It's the declivity that shapes our ends.

III:42

XI:97

Vna nocte quater possum: sed quattuor annis
si possum, peream, te Telesilla semel.

Simple Aveu

Four times a night, that's me, as a general thing;
but with you, Telesilla, damned
if I could make it once in four years of nights.

XI:97

XIV:151

Longa satis nunc sum; dulci sed pondere uenter
si tumeat, fiam tunc tibi zona breuis.

Words from a Sash

I'm long enough to be fashionable now,
but unless you're a careful girl,
sooner or later you'll find me all too short.

XIV:151

XII:56

Aegrotas uno decies aut saepius anno,
  nec tibi sed nobis hoc, Polycharme, nocet:
nam quotiens surgis, soteria poscis amicos.
  Sit pudor: aegrota iam, Polycharme, semel.

Dear Polycharmus:

Ten times a year, or more, you're sick in bed
with some sort of virus, but
it's your friends, not you, that get the misery.
They're the ones you expect to throw a party
every time you recover.
Pol, have a heart, we
beg you: go to bed sick once and for all.

XII: 56

II:87

Dicis amore tui bellas ardere puellas
qui faciem sub aqua, Sexte, natantis habes.

Valentine

You claim that all the pretties are panting for you:
for you, Fitts,
face of a drowned clown floating under water.

II:87

V:60

Adlatres licet usque nos et usque
et gannitibus inprobis lacessas,
certum est hanc tibi pernegare famam,
olim quam petis, in meis libellis
qualiscumque legaris ut per orbem.
nam te cur aliquis sciat fuisse?
ignotus pereas, miser, necesse est.
non derunt tamen hac in urbe forsan
unus uel duo tresue quattuorue
pellem rodere qui uelint caninam:
nos hac a scabie tenemus ungues.

To a Detractor

Yap-yap at me, you yap,
huff your stinking breath: you'll get
no fame from me, the look
of your name in my book, for all to see.

You exist, yap, you exist; but why
should the world know? Die,
cypher. Go down as you've lived, without recognition.
It's a big city,
and there may be a man, or two men, or even three,
with a taste for dead dog-flesh;
                                        as for me,
I'll keep my fingernails clean of your infection.

V:60

IX:33

Audieris in quo, Flacce, balneo plausum,
Maronis illic esse mentulam scito.

Lux et Veritas

You ask at the Baths why all this sudden applause?
It's their habit, Cabot.
Another Yale type has stepped out of his drawers.

IX:33

XII:65

Formonsa Phyllis nocte cum mihi tota
se praestitisset omnibus modis largam,
et cogitarem mane quod darem munus,
utrumne Cosmi, Nicerotis an libram,
an Baeticarum pondus acre lanarum,
an de moneta Caesaris decem flauos:
amplexa collum basioque tam longo
blandita quam sunt nuptiae columbarum,
rogare coepit Phyllis amphoram uini.

Phyllis Is a Straight Shooter

You know Phyllis? Yes, well,
I was over there last night, and I tell you
she sure spread herself!
                                        So this morning
I wanted to give her something extra, like
a flacon of No. 5, maybe? a couple of yards
of burlap leotard? five or ten bucks extra?
Anyhow, I asked her,
                                        and—believe it or not—
she took off on a standing jump & gave me a kiss
that damn near sprung my ankles,
                                                            and here
is what she asked me for:
                                                    1 bbl. of beer.

XII:65

XI:79

Ad primum decuma lapidem quod uenimus hora,
  arguimur lentae crimine pigritiae.
non est ista quidem, non est mea, sed tua culpa est
  misisti mulas qui mihi, Paete, tuas.

Remonstrance

Pete, I admit I was late. It took me ten hours
to cover a mile.
                It was not my fault, but yours:
Why did you lend me your car?

XI:79

VIII:10

Emit lacernas milibus decem Bassus
Tyrias coloris optimi. Lucrifecit.
'Adeo bene emit?' inquis. Immo non soluet.

Charge It, Please

Lowe just bought
a bolero-type pur-
ple overcoat
with laminated but-
tons and yellow twill.
Two bucks fif-
ty-seven.
            'What
a bargain!'
            Stet.
Lowe never yet
has paid a bill.

VIII:10

XII:12

Omnia promittis cum tota nocte bibisti,
  mane nihil praestas. Pollio, mane bibe.

To Pollio, Nocturnally Euphoric

Pollio, you'd give us the world
when you're falling-down drunk at midnight,
but at breakfast you can't remember.
Pollio, start drinking at breakfast.

XII:12

XII:16

Addixti, Labiene, tres agellos;
emisti, Labiene, tres cinaedos:
pedicas, Labiene, tres agellos.

Conversion

You sold your three little pastures, Labienus?
And you've bought three pretty slave boys, Labienus?
You still own three little pastures, Labienus.

XII: 16

II:88

Nil recitas et uis, Mamerce, poeta uideri.
  quidquid uis esto, dummodo nil recites.

To an Aspiring Colleague

You're dying to pass for a poet, Mamercus, yet
you never give public readings.

Pass for whatever you damn well please, so long
as you never give public readings.

II:88

VI:57

Mentiris fictos unguento, Phoebe, capillos
  et tegitur pictis sordida calua comis.
tonsorem capiti non est adhibere necesse:
  radere te melius spongea, Phoebe, potest.

Every Man His Own Absalom

With fictive locks and scented glue
you hide your dome: who's fooling who?

A haircut? That's a simple matter.
No clippers, please; just soap and water.

VI:57

III:51

Cum faciem laudo, cum miror crura manusque,
  dicere, Galla, soles 'Nuda placebo magis',
et semper uitas communia balnea nobis.
  Numquid, Galla, times ne tibi non placeam?

Aphrodite Katadyomene

Dear Francine, when I praise your knees,
  your face, your hands, your breast,
you blush and say, 'If you like these,
  you ought to see the rest!'

Yet at the Baths, when I swim near,
  you shun me utterly.
Fran, are you shy? or do you fear
  you'd have to blush for me?

III:51

XI:107

Explicitum nobis usque ad sua cornua librum
  et quasi perlectum, Septiciane, refers.
omnia legisti. Credo, scio, gaudeo, uerum est.
  perlegi libros sic ego quinque tuos.

To a Brother Poet

You send me back my books, Septician,
'read again & again', 'utterly memorized'.

Yes. I know. I'm glad. I even believe you.
That's exactly the way I read your last 5 vols.

XI:107

VII:73

Esquiliis domus est, domus est tibi colle Dianae,
  et tua patricius culmina uicus habet;
hinc uiduae Cybeles, illinc sacraria Vestae,
  inde nouum, ueterem prospicis inde Iouem.
dic ubi conueniam, dic qua te parte requiram:
  quisquis ubique habitat, Maxime, nusquam habitat.

'. . . Are Many Mansions'

That's a fine place you have on Beacon Hill, Max,
and that unlisted duplex out Huntington Avenue,
and the old homestead in Tewksbury.

From one you can see

the big gilt dome; the second
gives you an uninterrupted ecstatic view
of the Mother Church; the third
commands the County Poorhouse.

And you

invite me to dinner?

There?

There?

Or there?

Max, a man who lives everywhere

lives nowhere.

VII:73

IX:15

Inscripsit tumulis septem scelerata uirorum
se FECISSE Chloe. Quid pote simplicius?

On Chloë, a Widow Too Frequent

On each of the seven tombs of her seven husbands
you will find this plain inscription:
ERECTED BY CHLOE.

IX:15

II:38

Quid mihi reddat ager quaeris, Line, Nomentanus?
  Hoc mihi reddit ager: te, Line, non uideo.

Information Requested & Supplied

That farm of mine up country—what
does it get me, Linus? You want to know?
Linus, it gets me away from you.

II:38

IV:17

Facere in Lyciscam, Paule, me iubes uersus,
quibus illa lectis rubeat et sit irata.
O Paule, malus es: irrumare uis solus.

Epigram Reduced

You beg me to abuse your girl in print?
to bring a blush (if possible) to those cheeks?

Paul, Paul, you're simply being possessive.

IV: 17

XIV:175

Cur a te pretium Danae, regnator Olympi,
  accepit, gratis si tibi Leda dedit?

On a Painting of Danaë in the Golden Rain

Why put out cash for Danaë, Chairman of Heaven,
  when you could have Leda for nothing?

XIV: 175

XIV:180

Mutari melius tauro, pater optime diuum,
   tunc poteras Io cum tibi uacca fuit.

On a Painting of Europa and the Bull

A better time for bullish impersonation,
  God of gods, was when Iô heifered for you.

XIV:180

VII:9

Cum sexaginta numeret Cascellius annos,
  ingeniosus homo est: quando disertus erit?

Literary Query

Ætat. 60, our old friend Oldys is still
'a poet of promise'.
                                        When will he pay off?

VII:9

VI:24

Nil lasciuius est Charisiano:
Saturnalibus ambulat togatus.

Statement

D. Fitts is
  the lewdest man!
He'd wear full dress
  in a nudist camp.

VI:24

II:15

Quod nulli calicem tuum propinas
humane facis, Horme, non superbe.

'Take, Oh Take Those Lips Away'

You let no-one drink from your personal cup, Hormus,
when the toasts go round the table.
Haughtiness?
                    Hell, no.
Humanity.

II:15

XII:7

Toto uertice quot gerit capillos
annos si tot habet Ligeia, trima est.

Too Late for Herpicide

Count her years by the hairs on her head,
and Ligeia's
not yet ready for nursery school.

XII:7

III:53

Et uoltu poteram tuo carere
et collo manibusque cruribusque
et mammis natibusque clunibusque,
et, ne singula persequi laborem,
tota te poteram, Chloe, carere.

To Chloë

Take oh take that face away,
that neck away, those arms away,
hips and bottom, legs and breast—
Dear, must I catalogue the rest?
Take, Chloë, take yourself away.

III:53

III:80

De nullo quereris, nulli maledicis, Apici:
rumor ait linguae te tamen esse malae.

To Apicius, Whose Tastes Are Odd

You never speak ill of anyone, Apicius;
and yet, Apicius,
the story goes that you've a naughty tongue.

III:80

VII:94

Vnguentum fuerat, quod onyx modo parua gerebat:
olfecit postquam Papylus, ecce, garumst.

Papylus's Best Friends Won't Tell Him

This little onyx jar held a rare perfume
till Papylus sniffed it.
Now my rare perfume suggests a perturbèd polecat.

VII:94

III:87

Narrat te rumor, Chione, numquam esse fututam
  atque nihil cunno purius esse tuo.
tecta tamen non hac, qua debes, parte lauaris:
  si pudor est, transfer subligar in faciem.

To Chionë, Ambiguously Prudent

Intact? Aseptic, Chionë?
  For miles and miles around,
your peer for sheer pudicity
  is nowhere to be found.

Even at the Baths you swathe with care
  the cunning innocent place.
'Twere purer logic, dear, to wear
  your panties on your face.

III:87

III:90

Volt, non uolt dare Galla mihi, nec dicere possum,
quod uolt et non uolt, quid sibi Galla uelit.

Lines Written in Dejection Near a Hen-Coop

She will, she won't; she won't, she will;
  so what am I to do?
Will she, or won't she will until
  she won't? I think so, too.

III:90

III:28

Auriculam Mario grauiter miraris olere.
  Tu facis hoc: garris, Nestor, in auriculam.

A Double Valentine

You claim to be shocked, Ness, because Manny's ears
are dirty.
Why are you shocked? You've been talking to him.

III:28

I:35

Versus scribere me parum seueros
nec quos praelegat in schola magister,
Corneli, quereris: sed hi libelli,
tamquam coniugibus suis mariti,
non possunt sine mentula placere.
quid si me iubeas thalassionem
uerbis dicere non thalassionis?
quis Floralia uestit et stolatum
permittit meretricibus pudorem?
lex haec carminibus data est iocosis,
ne possint, nisi pruriant, iuuare.
quare deposita seueritate
parcas lusibus et iocis rogamus,
nec castrare uelis meos libellos.
Gallo turpius est nihil Priapo.

To a Censorious Critic

So my verse offends you.
'No taste,' you say, 'no dig-
nity,' as though the class-
room were my proper sphere.
My lines, Cornelius,
like husbands, have licence
to hone the pleasure point.
No stag-party ballad
goes to a psalm tune, your
Mardi-Gras whore would look
absurd frocked by Dior.
No; what I want in verse
is: scratch where you itch.
Then screw solemnity:
carnival's today. You'd
not castrate my poems,
I hope? Gelded Priá-
pus? There's obscenity!

I:35

XI:104

Vxor, uade foras aut moribus utere nostris:
  non sum ego nec Curius nec Numa nec Tatius.
me iucunda iuuant tractae per pocula noctes:
  tu properas pota surgere tristis aqua.
tu tenebris gaudes: me ludere teste lucerna
  et iuuat admissa rumpere luce latus.
fascia te tunicaeque obscuraque pallia celant:
  at mihi nulla satis nuda puella iacet.
basia me capiunt blandas imitata columbas:
  tu mihi das auiae qualia mane soles.
nec motu dignaris opus nec uoce iuuare
  nec digitis, tamquam tura merumque pares:
masturbabantur Phrygii post ostia serui
  Hectoreo quotiens sederat uxor equo,
et quamuis Ithaco stertente pudica solebat
  illic Penelope semper habere manum.
pedicare negas: dabat hoc Cornelia Graccho,
  Iulia Pompeio, Porcia, Brute, tibi;
dulcia Dardanio nondum miscente ministro
  pocula Iuno fuit pro Ganymede Ioui.
Si te delectat grauitas, Lucretia toto
  sis licet usque die, Laida nocte uolo.

A Marital Declaration

There's only one thing for it: put up
with my 'degenerate ways', as you call them, or
go home to Mama.
Admittedly, I'm not one
of those stern & rockbound types, homespun
whiskers, bores
bugling from pulpit and podium. When I drink
it's a long wet night for me; you go to bed
with a bumper of water at sunset. When I make love
I want every light on full blast; you insist
upon darkness,
a nightgown,
a wrapper,
& blankets—
(For me, who've never found
a naked girl naked enough!)
—Kissing? I like it,
but I like it as doves kiss, beaks ajar; you kiss
as though you were greeting your grandmother at breakfast.
A loving technic?
What a technic! Paralyzed, wordless, never so much
as a curious hand:
your hand's reserved, I take it,
for Ladies' Day at the altar.
Ah the old days
when his wife rode Hector, that bucking gay horse,

and the Phrygian slaves
played with themselves outside the bedroom door!
Those halcyon days
when Ulysses snorted asleep, yet wise Penelope
employed her instructed fingers!

Those blessed days
when good Cornelia gave (what you deny)
herself reversed to her Gracchus!

and Julia to Pompey!

and
Portia, Brutus, to you!

when Juno herself
was Ganymede enough for Lord Jupiter!

All right.

This is my point: I can bear Lucretia by daylight,
but at night
I want a Laïs in my bed who knows her business.

XI:104

IV:72

Exigis ut donem nostros tibi, Quinte, libellos.
  Non habeo, sed habet bibliopola Tryphon.
'Aes dabo pro nugis et emam tua carmina sanus?
  non' inquis 'faciam tam fatue.' Nec ego.

To Quintus, One of Many

Each time I get out a new book of poems, Quintus,
you expect a free copy. Yet there are bookstores.

'What? Pay good money for the stuff you write?
Do I look feeble-minded?'

No, Quintus. Do I?

IV:72

I:10

Petit Gemellus nuptias Maronillae
et cupit et instat et precatur et donat.
Adeone pulchra est? Immo foedius nil est.
Quid ergo in illa petitur et placet? Tussit.

Society Note

Bankrupt Jim's after rich old Milly.
  He sighs, begs, charges up gifts. It's tough!
—'This Milly's a beaut, then?'
                                        Don't be silly.
  —'So what's the attraction?'
                                        A hacking cough.

I:10

XI:85

Sidere percussa est subito tibi, Zoile, lingua
dum lingis. Certe, Zoile, nunc futues.

On Zoïlus, a Linguist

Paralysis engaged the tongue
  of Zoïlus, I grieve to say,
as he was testing beauty's bung.
  Now he must try the triter way.

XI:85

X:91

Omnes eunuchos habet Almo, nec arrigit ipse:
  et queritur pariat quod sua Polla nihil.

Clinical Note

Though they're all eunuchs in his household and
he himself is the eunuchest of all,
poor Elmer fails to understand
what he likes to call
the morose immultiplicability
of his wife Pol.

x:91

V:47

Numquam se cenasse domi Philo iurat, et hoc est:
non cenat quotiens nemo uocauit eum.

Penny-Pincher

Phil swears to God that he never dines at home,
and that's no lie:
when he's not invited out, he goes to bed.

v:47

X:84

Miraris quare dormitum non eat Afer?
accumbat cum qua, Caeciliane, uides.

Why Mr Coons Reads Novels All Night

Cecil, you find it strange that our friend Coons
sits up so late at night?
Take another (& more thoughtful) look, dear Cecil,
at Mrs Coons.

x:84

III:96

Lingis, non futuis meam puellam
et garris quasi moechus et fututor.
Si te prendero, Gargili, tacebis.

To a Bragging Rival

You don't lay her, you lick her, you sick fraud,
and you tell the whole damn town you're her lover.

Gargilius, I swear to God,
if I catch you at it you'll be tongue-tied for ever.

III:96

XII:46

Difficilis facilis iucundus acerbus es idem:
nec tecum possum uiuere nec sine te.

To One of Shifting Moods

You're balky, pliant, merry, morose, all at once.
For me there's no living with you
or without you.

XII:46

XI:35

Ignotos mihi cum uoces trecentos,
quare non ueniam uocatus ad te
miraris quererisque litigasque.
Solus ceno, Fabulle, non libenter.

Civitas Solitudo

Fabullus, you invite 300
characters to dinner, not a one
I've ever so much as heard of, and
you give me hell for turning you down.
Why, Fabullus?
I simply don't like dining alone.

XI:35

VII:75

Vis futui gratis cum sis deformis anusque.
res perridicula est: uis dare nec dare uis.

To an Elderly but Still Enthusiastic Lady

You're old, you're uglier than a hake,
and you want to get taken for free? Wake
up, woman, kick in your share:
the giver without a gift is bare.

VII:75

VIII:69

Miraris ueteres, Vacerra, solos
nec laudas nisi mortuos poetas.
Ignoscas petimus: Vacerra, tanti
non est, ut placeam tibi, perire.

To His Critics

You puff the poets of other days,
  the living you deplore.
Spare me the accolade: your praise
  is not worth dying for.

VIII:69

I:117

Occurris quotiens, Luperce, nobis,
'Vis mittam puerum' subinde dicis,
'cui tradas epigrammaton libellum,
lectum quem tibi protinus remittam?'
Non est quod puerum, Luperce, uexes.
longum est si uelit ad Pirum uenire,
et scalis habito tribus sed altis.
quod quaeris propius petas licebit.
Argi nempe soles subire Letum:
contra Caesaris est forum taberna
scriptis postibus hinc et inde totis,
omnis ut cito perlegas poetas.
illinc me pete. nec roges Atrectum—
hoc nomen dominus gerit tabernae—:
de primo dabit alteroue nido
rasum pumice purpuraque cultum
denarîs tibi quinque Martialem.
'Tanti non es' ais? Sapis, Luperce.

Any Author to Any Friend

Every time I run into you, Luke,
you ask me: 'Look,
how about my sending that boy of mine
over to your place
for a copy of that book you just got out?
I'll read it,' you tell me, 'and
send it right back. Okay?'
—Just fine.
But on the other hand,
I live pretty far out, and there's no point
in going to all that trouble & making your boy
climb three flights up to my pad.
Look, Luke,
I've thought of a simpler way.
You know that paper store on the Square
across from Widener? Books everywhere,
poems all over the place. Well,
you just walk in & say: 'Please,
Felix,'—his name is Felix—'will you sell
me a copy of M. V. Martial's latest vol.?'
Will he? I should hope to tell
you he will! all
spick & span and bound in deep cerise.
Price? Three ninety-nine.
—'Three ninety-hell!
You aren't worth that much.'
—There you hit it, pal.

I:117

Index of Latin First Lines